La Ventana

Forest Meditations

Ryan G

For M.L.,Y.G., B.K., P.P., M.M.M. & the ones I've lost with love.

She is the forest.

I.

Here, I cry.

It has been a long time since I have felt so whole.

The fullness bubbles up and over

My tear ducts set it free to flow

and well up all over again.

The crow tells me to forgive myself

for my cowardice in the dark.

Reluctantly, I listen.

4 redwoods offer their curves to

comfort my heavy eyes and graciously,

I accept.

II.

I am enjoying myself here.

I know you're surprised.

You use your hands, and so do I

My talons are black like the earth,

like the charred trees.

I wish I were less vain.

Thank God you love me anyway.

I imagine you looking for me,

following my scent, a wavering trail through the oak,

clover and creek bed,

touching the same trunks as I,

stopping to gaze up at the canopy in the

same selfless awe.

III.

I have so much love for her

Love for the unattached giving of herself

Her quiet, proud sustainability

Her acceptance of me.

"I'm exhausted." I say aloud

"I know" says the creek. "Sit here with me."

I stumble over washed out forest bed and exposed roots.

"Where?"

"Here," says the cluster of redwoods closest to the creek. "There

is shade between us."

I feel clumsy, and long and spindly limbs, but the redwoods do

not judge.

The ferns bow in greeting.

I place myself between the trees on a soft bed of eucalyptus leaves.

The catacombs where the redwoods meet provides a comforting

breeze of damp, cool air.

I can't think of a better place to write.

IV.

One of the things I would like to do most here is yell.

Disturb the unselfconscious peace with my own chaos.

Infantile as it may be,

I wish to fill the air with my sound.

The trees would not mind,

they know the sounds of the earth itself and any human noise

disperses itself up, in and away.

A thin, flat echo amongst the undetectably low groans and sighs

of earth.

It's mocking me, bringing my feeble ego to the surface and letting

each layer wither and blow away.

I am left with the remembrance of my smallness.

Let to do and feel what I may.

The emaciation of my creative power is restored here.

This is what I needed.

I wonder how long I have starved, it now seems like half my

lifetime.

Only now do I know how vacant I have been. Like the hollows of

the redwood roots.

I am reminded of it being said (falsely) that only the outermost

parts of the trees are alive.

What a liberty of existence, solely on the surface.

I hope to find the exoskeleton of a cicada here,

in remembrance.

V.

It is here,

It is everywhere.

It was in me, but I forgot.

VI.

//Fallen Tree//

Knock me down

Wash me away

I am cored

I am cured

VII.

//You can't make a spider hurry//

Bless the spiders, for they live in paradise.

"How do you weave silk?" I ask them, in their villas in the

grooves of the redwood bark.

Spiders are painfully shy creatures. The quiet type.

"Wait here," one piped up, in a sliver of a whisper.

My arachnophobia is as acute as it is irrational, but I leaned in

closer to the little voice.

"I'll show you."

VIII.

I wish you were here.

I would show you the barren rocky river bed

Take a picture of you in the heart of the damp old redwood stump.

You and I belong in the forest.

I am your ivy

Nourish me and I will flourish.

IX.

Everything is so lush here,

Does it know it's fate?

X.

She is fearless

(I wish to be like her)

She is just as vain as I am.

XI.

I am gratified by the relieving of my fluids and excrement

There is room for me here,

I can finally relax.

I question every seemingly relaxed state before.

XII.

I like the charred trees best

They are survivors and black like me.

XIII.

You ask me why the flys don't bother me and it's because I'm

flattered that they like my smell.

XIV.

I admire the stab wounds in a stump and apologize,

I would like to know what that feels like too.

XV.

I am just as exhibitionistic and reserved as she is

There are hips here,

Hips, vulvas, long legs and uncircumcised cocks and massive

asses here.

She is perverse, damp, lush, odorous and uninhibited.

She is beautiful,

She knows.

She turns me on,

& relishes it. She humbles me,

and shows me things I have never seen before.

I thank her.

Her lushness makes me hard,

I am uncertain of whether to laugh, cry or orgasm on the spot, and

begin to think of ways to do all at once.

She lets me see her, I thank her.

I get the nerve to speak. I need to.

"I've lost some things," I tell her, tears in my eyes.

"I have too." She says.

XVI.

I am wild here, just like she is.

I cackle like a banshee, urinate in every clearing and push him

inside of me as deep as he can go.

Since living with her, he has been a much better lover.

She is proud of me, and shows me how to catch the light with my

silk.

I am the best I have ever been here.

She agrees.

I would like to take care of her, in vain.

She doesn't need me.

I, once more, become insecure with myself.

I want to make things right.

"I'll go to school," I say. "I'll get my degree."

"What?"

"I'll stop loving to suffer so much," I continue."I want to make

things right."

She laughs at me, in gurgling bubbles.

In honor of The Ventana Wilderness

For sharing herself with me.